WHO WAS ROBERT JOHNSON?

Born a man-child where the ragged land scratched its underbelly

Raised on a diddley bow and harmonica

Saw the world with two eyes, one woeful, out of a beautiful face

Hid behind the names Robert Spencer, Robert Dodd, Robert Dusty,
Robert Lonnie, Robert Saxton

Wore a three-piece pinstripe suit in Miss'ippi mud rut rain

Liked the mischief of open A, capoed at the 2nd fret

Thumb-picked, finger-picked, straight-picked or rode bareback
the barrelhouse blues

Set down octaves deep in the heat of Arkansas back country

Drank twelve men's shares of Ten High

Watched shimmering dresses slit with desire

Left a hundred women in a hundred towns and half a hundred
husbands shouting *Fool, you*

Lived, loved, gone by breakfast

Outwalked a footfall of walking musicians

Jangled the nerves of the railroad bulls

Enveloped in a legend

Lionized beyond belief

Approved on a postage stamp

The Life of Blues Legend Robert Johnson

BLACK

J. Patrick Lewis

CAT

Illustrations by Gary Kelley

BONE

Creative Editions Mankato

Text copyright © 2006 J. Patrick Lewis

Illustrations copyright © 2006 Gary Kelley

Published in 2006 by Creative Editions

123 South Broad Street, Mankato, MN 56001 USA

Creative Editions is an imprint of The Creative Company.

Designed by Rita Marshall

Printed in Italy

Library of Congress Cataloging-in-Publication Data

Lewis, J. Patrick.

Black cat bone / by J. Patrick Lewis ; illustrator, Gary Kelley.

ISBN-13 : 978-1-56846-194-6

1. Johnson, Robert, d. 1938—Juvenile poetry. 2. African American musicians—Juvenile poetry. 3. Blues musicians—Juvenile poetry. 4. Mississippi—Juvenile poetry. 5. Children's poetry, American. 6. Blues (Music)—Texts. I. Kelley, Gary. II. Title.

PS3562.E9465B527 2006   811'.54—dc22   2005052298

First edition 9 8 7 6 5 4 3 2 1

For the people of New Orleans and southern Mississippi—J.P.L.

For my dad, who raised me in a houseful of music—G.K.

FOREWORD

Robert Johnson was born into Mississippi poverty in 1911. The son of a sharecropper but no fan of fieldwork, Robert developed a love of music at an early age. He started out playing the Jew's harp and harmonica but soon put them down in favor of the guitar and apprenticed himself to Ike Zinnerman, an excellent blues guitarist from Alabama. Robert quickly learned to sing the blues, taking notes from such other blues greats as Son House, Charley Patton, and Willie Brown.

Although Robert played with many musicians, he was a loner by nature and lived a life chronicled largely by fleeting facts, hearsay, and tall tales. He spread his music all over Mississippi and Arkansas, usually in small roadside establishments where people ate, drank, and danced. It was said that Robert's greatness came from a midnight pact he struck with the devil at a Mississippi crossroad, exchanging his soul for musical immortality.

Robert recorded twenty-nine songs during his short lifetime, only one of which, "Terraplane Blues," became a hit. But his performances made a lasting impression on all those fortunate enough to witness them, generating lasting stories of his splendor. When Robert died at the age of twenty-seven, his name became mythical.

Many musicians over the last seven decades have sung Robert's praises. Guitarist Keith Richards said, "When I first heard him, I was hearing two guitars, and it took me a long time to realize he was actually doing it all by himself." Blues artist Bonnie Raitt added, "[His] music sent me reeling. I couldn't even imagine how someone could play the guitar the way he did and sing at the same time."

Through poetry and illustration, the following pages peer into Robert's life, death, music, and legend, illuminating the rise and legacy of the man some have called "The Godfather of the Blues."

The long fuse snaking through Europe

to World War I twitches for a spark.

Hiram Bingham stumbles onto the Lost City

of the Incas. The Triangle Shirtwaist Company

ignites like straw, killing 146 helpless

women working under inhuman conditions.

Calbraith Rodgers flies the first coast-to-coast

U.S. flight in 49 days, 69 stops and 13 crash

landings—they pay him five dollars a mile.

And on May 8th, in Hazelhurst, Mississippi,

a misbegotten dot on a hardscrabble map,

halfway between whatnot and nowhere,

the clocks are wound to revolution.

A devil wind lifts the skirts of the South.

Robert Johnson is born, and later baptized

by the grace of the black gods of sound.

1911

ROBERT WAS BORN IN 1911.

YOUNG ROBERT

He was destined for legend.

"Too lazy," Dusty Willis said,
"To stand behind a mule
Plowin' days into a year."
"I ain't nobody's fool,"

Young Robert said. "Stepdaddy,
What you bust a gut to get
Ain't nothin' from the bossman
But a hundred dollar debt.

"I'd rather play harmonica
Than agitate a mule,
I'd rather wake to nightmares than
Dream my way through school."

Sixteen is all she was the night she died.

Virginia might have made an honest man

Of Robert. But his walking days began

The fateful evening Death embraced his bride

THE NIGHT VIRGINIA DIED

And stillborn child. How could a body bear

To deal with the anguish he was dealt?

How can we say exactly what he felt

Who've never known such chasms of despair?

But nothing could have held him in a place

With nothing left to save of saving grace.

OR LIFE AS A FAMILY MAN.

DISAPPEARED

Met a woman, what a woman,
She was ten years older,
Callie laughin', Callie cryin'
Heavy on his shoulder.

Loved that woman, left that woman
On account o' she was down.
Folks'll swear they saw him ridin'
On a whisper outta town.

CONGREGATION BLUES

Black preacher man's words come smoking

out of the hymn-ridden South like a Delta fire

the blues, the blues, why they be nothin'

but a cornfield beggar's eulogy

a six-bit floozy on a two-bit holiday

an undertaker's gospel sung by a gravedigger

Lady La-la tricked out like Paintnail Sally

a hoodoo curse rattlin' black cat bones

   from the other side

brilliantine rubbed on the rails to Gomorrha

the blues, the blues, why they be makin' Jesus blush

And the hallelujah chorus sings,

Amen, Amen, Amen

YOUNG ROBERT LIKED THE BLUES.

Jook joint's about to come alive!
It's like a bee outside a hive;
And when the hive begins to hum,
It's like a dim and distant drum;
And when the drum begins to beat,
It's like a circus down the street;
And when the street begins to fill,
It's like a sudden summer chill;
And just as summer simmers down,

It's like the fireworks over town.
Don't matter what the preachers say—
This congregation's here to stay
'Cause when the jook joint comes alive
Is when the Delta blues arrive!

JOOK JOINT SATURDAY NIGHT

THE RUCKUS OF COUNTRY SHINDIGS,

WHAT SON HOUSE SAW

One night in Banks, Mississippi,

the jick was flowin', the shack

was hoppin' to what Willie and I

were puttin' down. In walks Robert.

We started to laugh seein'

the little man's backstrapped

guitar—a wood-bodied Stella—

like maybe he's gonna play it

in front of everybody. Like they

gonna stop, say, Hold on,

it's the new Charley Patton.

Wasn't that long ago,

a year? Two years?

I told him, *Beat it, boy,*

you'll get stepped on.

Stick to the harmonica.

Gimme your seat a minute, Son,

He says. And I'm thinkin',

Here comes shame in a buggy.

He goes to pickin' notes ungodly

From a land unknown, singin'

like a blackbird possessed.

We stood there dumb as dirt,

mouths catchin' flies.

Little Robert grew up fast.

AT THE CROSSROAD,

"Mister Johnson

I see you look to buyin'

Mister Johnson

That all you want is Fame?

Mister Johnson

Now what you got to offer?

Mister Johnson

Salvation is my name

With a rhythm on a riff

That's practically God

Oh Lord, I'm a pure

Undivining rod

I'm a flickerin' candle

With the blackest light

I'm the darkest angel

And I own the night

Mister Johnson

That instrument you got there

Mister Johnson

It's Lucifer's guitar

Mister Johnson

I'll tune it for you, baby

Mister Johnson

They won't know who you are

I'm a cutthroat seller,

The Magician of Deal

Who can stoke sweet fire

That'll make you feel

Like a hothouse flower

On double defrost

Who won't give a nickel

For the petals it lost

Mister Johnson

You slink on back to livin'

Mister Johnson

In devil-may-care control

Mister Johnson

Don't thank me for the favor

Mister Johnson

I thank you for your soul"

HIGHWAYS 61 AND 49

SOME SAY IT WAS THE DEVIL'S HAND

Cross Road Blues (take 2)

I went to the crossroad
    fell down on my knees
I went to the crossroad
    fell down on my knees
Asked the Lord above "Have mercy
    save poor Bob, if you please"

Mmmmm, standin' at the crossroad
    I tried to flag a ride
Standin' at the crossroad
    I tried to flag a ride
Didn't nobody seem to know me
    everybody pass me by

Mmmm, the sun goin' down, boy
    dark gon' catch me here
Oooo ooee eeee
    boy, dark gon' catch me here
I haven't got no lovin' sweet woman that
    love and feel my care

You can run, you can run
    tell my friend-boy Willie Brown
You can run
    tell my friend-boy Willie Brown
Lord, that I'm standin' at the crossroad, babe
    I believe I'm sinkin' down

lyrics by Robert Johnson

THE BLUESMAN'S LAMENT

What on earth you do with
This Robert Johnson kid.
You tell him you're the cook pot,
He says, I'll be the lid.

Only one track runs through
This Robert Johnson's brain.
Folks say you make the window.
He'll say, I'll be the pane.

So you become a part of
A Robert Johnson dream.
Imagine you're the coffee;
Imagine he's the cream.

Then something funny happens
To Robert Johnson's game
When you become the candle
And he becomes the flame.

And you become late winter,
And he becomes the spring,
And they pronounce you jester
While they declare him king.

THAT STRUMMED UP HIS FAME.

Was you layin' licks in Lula

Like they said you was last night?

Maybe it was Coahoma,

Seems I heard about a fight.

MYSTERY MAN

So the story goes in Tchula,

With Willie Brown so sweet,

You tore the rafters from the shack

'Fore sunlight hit the street.

In Yazoo City, Son House said,

You made that wood box sing.

Johnny Shines said, Nah, was Beulah

Where the boy did *every*thing.

Was it you or only shadow

Jitterbuggin' Hollandale?

Ain't a stone detective livin'

Who knows your every tale.

RUMORS SWIRLED AROUND ROBERT

MOVIN' OUT MOVIN' ON

I got me the sugar fever, boys—
Ain't Dixie Dew or beer.
It's blowin' out of my guitar
To candy the atmosphere.
You gotta heap o' good nothin', boys,
And nothin' 'on' keep me here.

Travelin' somewhere, whistlin' train,
Bus or rumble seat,
I'm movin' out 'n' movin' on
To a house way down Serenity Street.

Love's shakin' for the takin', boys,
Can't get too much o' love.
Jook joint tonight's lined wall to wall
With pigeons—where's the dove?
The blues they color mystery you
Can't never get 'nuf of.

Travelin' Mississippi delta,
Where the moon and midnight meet,
I'm movin' out 'n' movin' on
Until I get to Serenity Street.

Some days play out unlucky, boys,
Some days you get your fill
Of whittled-to-splinter odds on backs
Of twenty dollar bills,
But long's I own a pick guitar,
Nothin' 'on' keep me still.

Travelin' light, this suitcase full
Of livin's bittersweet,
I'm moving' out 'n' movin' on
To a place they call Serenity Street.

BLUES

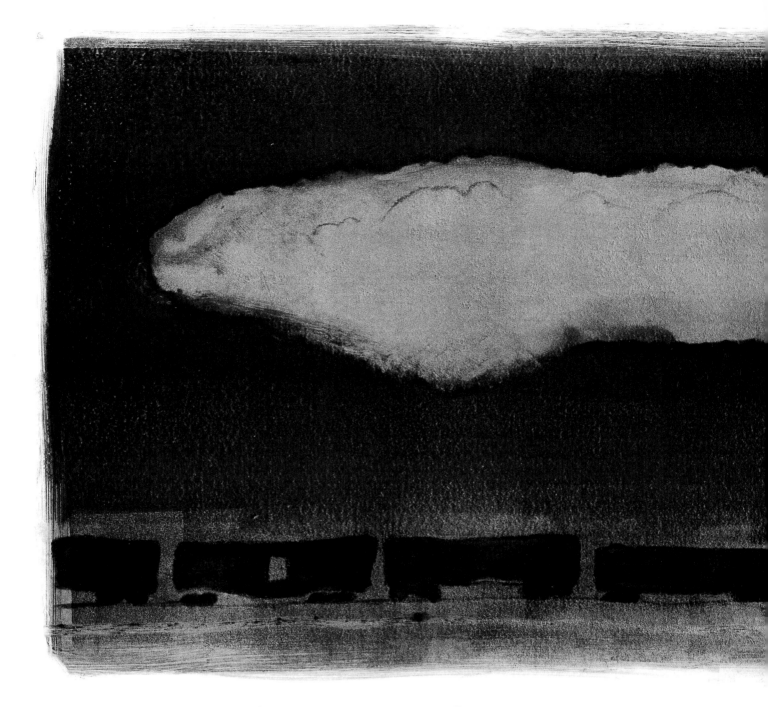

excerpt from Sweet Home Chicago

Oh, baby, don't you want to go
Oh, baby, don't you want to go
Back to the land of California
　　to my sweet home Chicago

Now one and one is two
　　two and two is four
I'm heavy loaded baby
　　I'm booked, I gotta go
Cryin', baby

honey, don't you want to go
Back to the land of California
to my sweet home Chicago

Now two and two is four
four and two is six
You gon' keep monkeyin' 'round here friend-boy,
you gon' get your business all in a trick
But I'm cryin', baby
honey, don't you want to go
Back to the land of California
to my sweet home Chicago

lyrics by Robert Johnson

In San Antonio, 1936,

He picks "Cross Road Blues"—

"Trying to flag a ride."

You can't help but notice

The peculiar way he slides.

He faces the wall, alone.

Suddenly—no one knows how—

He rediscovers sound.

Mexican boys trying their luck

Marvel at such beautiful hands

Flying off like a pair of swallows.

FIRST RECORDING SESSION

Showcasing his signature style,

He astonishes the air

With "Terraplane Blues,"

His only hit, skittering out

Into the musical world,

Its octaves in flames.

excerpt from **Terraplane Blues**

And I feel so lonesome
    you hear me when I moan
When I feel so lonesome
    you hear me when I moan
Who been drivin' my Terraplane
    for you since I been gone

I'd said I flash your lights, mama
    your horn won't even blow
(Somebody's been runnin' my batteries
    down on this machine)
I even flash my lights, mama
    this horn won't even blow
Got a short in this connection

hoo-well, babe, it's way down below
I'm 'on' h'ist your hood, mama
     I'm bound to check your oil
I'm gon' h'ist your hood, mama-mmmm
     I'm bound to check your oil
I got a woman that I'm lovin'
     way down in Arkansas

Now, you know the coils ain't even buzzin'
     little generator won't get the spark
Motor's in bad condition,
     you gotta have these batteries charged
But I'm cryin', please
     Pleas-hease don't do me wrong
Who been drivin' my Terraplane now for
     you-hoo since I been gone

lyrics by Robert Johnson

WOMEN LYING AWAKE

Long after love,
It's 3 a.m.,
When Robert shies
Away from them,

Strange women who
Have known him for
One night, or two,
And know the score.

He'd rather not
Awaken them.
He's searching for
A missing gem:

An undiscovered
Mythic chord
His fingers have
Not yet explored.

Guitar's his heaven
Come to ground—
His fingers slide
But make no sound.

Still, women toss
In restless sleep,
Awake, a one-eyed
Watch they keep.

When Robert hears
The women turn,
He hides the magic
Moves they'd learn.

Down in Greenwood, Mississippi, where the jook joints 'lectrify,

All that hoppin', screamin', sweatin' like to fricassee the sky.

When Honeyboy and Sonny Boy and Robert tore the blues,

Hot dancers ripped the evening, couple of 'em bust a fuse.

They say Robert took to flirtin' with the houseman's lovely wife.

Witnesses said it was certain he was flirtin' with his life.

Man handed him a whiskey pint that had a broken seal,

But Sonny Boy, he threw it down, "No way. It's a dirty deal."

"Don't ever knock free liquor out of Robert Johnson's hand,"

Said Robert. Then a second pint appeared. "You understand?"

So it goes, the slant-told tale of the night he took the bait

When the houseman poisoned Robert and the devil told his fate.

THREE FORKS

A TALL TALE ABOUT

Have you ever heard that tall a tale?
        Who knows what to believe?
Which part of Robert's legacy
        Biographers like to weave

Is absolutely true? Or false?
        No one can really say.
The night he died the devil might
        Have been three states away.

How he can occupy your mind,
        That lone tormented soul.
Some go so far to say that he's
        What started rock 'n' roll.

Whatever else the truth may be,
        Let books say this of him:
In dictionaries of the blues,
        Robert's the synonym.

A SHORT MAN

His passing spawned stories;

Greyhound buses rolling by like highway-hammered ships—
Get your ticket. Destination: The apocalypse.

Robert, always dressed to kill, princely to the bone,
Passin' strangers achin' just to hear his livelong moan.

THE LONG RIDE

His grave? Some say it's in Payne Chapel over Quitto way.
Or Greenwood's Little Zion Church. Some say there's hell to pay.

Some say they buried Robert by the roadside where he died
So he could get back on that Greyhound. Take it for a ride.

EVEN HIS BURIAL BECAME MYSTERY.

Superman flies onto his first comic book.

Oil bubbles up in Saudi Arabia.

Orson Welles' *The War of the Worlds* invades

every panicked radio along the eastern seaboard.

The Spanish Civil War rages on. Filming starts

on *The Wizard of Oz*. At New York City's

Carnegie Hall, John Hammond's *Spirituals*

To Swing concert explodes with African chants,

the Count Basie Band, boogie-woogie,

New Orleans jazz, hot gospel, stride piano,

harmonica instrumentals, Big Bill Broonzy's

blues. The audience hears the ghost of Robert

Johnson, four months gone, easing out

of a Victrola phonograph at center stage—

the entire concert suddenly enveloped

by the man who was not there.

1938

BUT HIS GHOST CONTINUED PLAYING.

A VOICE FROM THE GRAVE

"I lie here under
    The world I used to walk,
Where death is home to silence,
    But I can hear the talk.

"It seems a pity   "And once it's written,

   To lose the pedigree.   The history of the blues,

They've heard a hundred rappers   They'll cheer a dead man's genius.

      But haven't heard of me.   Never ask them whose."

HIS LEGACY STILL LIVES.

ENDNOTES

Who Was Robert Johnson?: According to almost every knowledgeable source, he was the greatest country blues artist who ever lived. Beyond that lies conjecture. At one extreme, jazz historian Rudi Blesh offers an overheated description of Robert's song "Hell Hound on My Trail" as typically "full of evil, surcharged with the terror of one alone among the moving unseen shapes of the night" (Davis, p. 94). But as Robert's friend and fellow guitarist Johnny Shines tells it, when playing for money, Robert was as happy singing "Yes, Sir, That's My Baby" or "My Blue Heaven" as anything remotely satanic (Wald, p. 118).

1911: The extraordinary life and times of Robert Johnson are rife with ambiguity and uncertainty. He was probably born on May 8, 1911, the eleventh child of Julia Major Dodds and Charles Dodds. He was illegitimate, his real father a plantation worker named Noah Johnson. Due to a land dispute, Charles Dodds fled Mississippi for Tennessee under a new surname, Spencer. Julia tried in vain to reunite the family. Eventually, the distant Dodds family accepted Robert, who spent his early years in Memphis. He rejoined his mother in the area of Robinsonville, Mississippi, in 1918 or 1920 and was raised by her and her new husband, Will "Dusty" Willis.

Young Robert: Robert's stepfather, Dusty Willis, was a sharecropper. In Willis's eyes, Robert was a shiftless no-account because he refused to get behind a plow and take up the life of a bossman's farmer. Although his mother and Willis raised him to manhood, the two men never got along.

The Night Virginia Died: In his youth, Robert played guitar most of his waking hours, but when he married Virginia Travis in Penton, Mississippi, in February 1929, he had not yet considered himself a musician. They lived with Robert's relatives on a Robinsonville plantation. By all accounts, he was a doting soon-to-be father in the summer of 1929. But Mrs. Robert Johnson and her baby died during childbirth in April 1930.

Congregation Blues: Despite what Northern upwardly mobile blacks might have thought, Southern churchgoers blamed Satan for seducing would-be Christians with the "devil's instruments." Such evil was easily allied to the "black arts" of voodoo and hoodoo, both held to be beneath contempt by respectable, working class blacks. Sin and superstition came packaged in a guitar.

Jook Joint Saturday Night: Dictionaries offer *juke* as the correct spelling, but it was always *jook* in the black community. A jook joint was often a rural convenience store converted to entertainment purposes ("Saturday night balls") that included the blues, dancing, and gambling. In some cases, a jook might operate every night of the week.

Disappeared: In May 1931, Robert married Calletta "Callie" Craft, a twice-wed mother of three. The couple kept their marriage a secret and moved north to the Delta town of Clarksdale, Mississippi. Callie fell ill within a year, and Robert abandoned her.

What Son House Saw: This coming-of-musical-age story highlights Robert's rise to respectability in the blues world. Son House and Willie Brown were so impressed by the young man's sudden leap to genius that they both admitted he had surpassed them in ability and appeal. He could be friendly or reserved, bashful or outgoing—a bundle of contradictions. Bluesman Robert Lockwood Jr., whose mother became Robert's regular girlfriend, called him "a strange dude" but praised him for his willingness to teach a young man everything he knew about the guitar.

At the Crossroad, Highways 61 and 49: Here is where the myth was born, grew wings, and took flight. Many people who know little about the blues can recite the legend of Robert Johnson's alleged pact with the devil. A young man living on a plantation in rural Mississippi, he took his burning desire to play the guitar out to this Crossroad one midnight, and there he met the devil himself in the form of a large black man. Satan tuned Robert's guitar, handed it back to him, and within a year's time, Robert became the king of the Delta blues. The cost: Robert's everlasting soul.

The Bluesman's Lament: "Cutting heads" referred to a kind of street competition in which blues musicians would stand on opposite corners and see whose music drew the largest crowd. There came a time when Robert's fame led his playing partners to claim that they were Robert Johnson because they knew his name alone would attract an audience.

Mystery Man: Quite apart from his alleged Faustian bargain with the devil, Robert was musically indebted to many of his blues contemporaries. He idolized Delta recording artist Lonnie Johnson (no relation), even going so far as to introduce himself occasionally as Robert Lonnie. Scrapper Blackwell, Skip James, and Kokomo Arnold left their distinguished marks on him. Ike Zinnerman more than anyone else was Robert's true mentor. Zinnerman claimed to have learned guitar in the graveyard at midnight while sitting atop tombstones. He was Robert's guitar encyclopedia, and he taught him how to mimic any style.

Movin' Out Movin' On Blues: According to his friend Johnny Shines, "Robert was a guy, you could wake him up anytime and he was ready to go. Say, for instance, you had come from Memphis and go [sic] to Helena [Arkansas], and we'd play there all night probably and lay down to sleep the next morning, and you hear a train. You say, 'Robert, I hear a train; let's catch it.' He wouldn't exchange no words with you; he's just ready to go.... I was just, matter of fact, tagging along" (Welding, p. 30).

First Recording Session: By 1936, Robert sought out H.C. Speir, a Jackson, Mississippi, furniture dealer and talent agent for many Mississippi blues singers. Speir contacted Ernie Oertle, an agent for the ARC Company, who arranged Robert's debut recording date in San Antonio's Gunter Hotel. When his turn to perform was called, Robert faced the wall, hesitating a long while. Some blamed it on his shyness; others said he was either hiding his slide moves or trying to maximize the acoustic effects. Whatever the reason, it added to his mystique. Over three days, he recorded several sides, the most commercially successful being "Terraplane Blues." He recorded again in Dallas seven months later.

Women Lying Awake: Robert's magnetism and good looks earned him a wicked reputation as a ladies' man. He would often arrive in a town and choose the ugliest woman he could find because he knew she was probably unattached. "Women, to Robert, were like motel or hotel rooms," Johnny Shines once said. "Even if he used them repeatedly he left them where he found them.... He preferred older women in their thirties over the younger ones, because the older ones would pay his way" (Wald, pp. 122-123). His fondness for women led to trouble with jealous husbands and boyfriends. It would also lead to his death.

Three Forks: The accounts of Robert's night of destiny are conflicting. Most claim that it took place in August 1938 at a Mississippi jook joint. David "Honeyboy" Edwards and John Lee "Sonny Boy" Williamson, who played with him that night, said his connection to a local woman had gone beyond flirting. Her jealous husband enticed Robert to drink from an open and tainted whiskey bottle—not a difficult task considering Robert's love for liquor. Overcome with nausea, he went outside and was seen crawling around on all fours, foaming at the mouth like a mad dog. Exactly how long he lived after his poisoning is in dispute. Transported to a Greenville boarding house fifteen miles away, he lay sick for several days, finally sweating the poison out of his system. But he caught pneumonia as a result and, most believe, died on August 16. Later, Robert's mother would say, "When I went in where he at, he layin' up in bed with his guitar crost his breast. Soon's he saw me, he say, 'Mama, you all I been waitin' for. Here,' he say, and he give me his guitar, 'take and hang this thing on the wall, 'cause I done pass all that by. That what got me messed up, Mama. It's the devil's instrument, just like you said. And I don't want it no more.' And he died while I was hangin' his guitar on the wall" (Lomax, p. 15).

A Tall Tale About a Short Man: What remains of the man and the myth that engulfed him is his music. Tall tales of Robert's life and exploits can monopolize any conversation about him, but in the end, it is his legacy of songs that will endure.

The Long Ride: If Robert's life is shadowed in myth, so too is his death and eventual burial. Near the former Three Forks Store, guitar picks and coins festoon his headstone, "Robert Johnson—Resting in the Blues." A second stone just north of Greenwood—and most likely his actual burial site—bears Robert's own handwritten message: "Jesus of Nazareth, King of Jerusalem. I know that my Redeemer liveth and that He will call me from the Grave." However, his June 1937 Dallas recording of "Me and the Devil Blues" included these words: "You may bury my body, ooh, down by the highway side/So my old evil spirit, can catch a Greyhound bus and ride."

1938: John Hammond's *Spirituals To Swing* concert, featuring black music of every form, was the first of its kind. A wealthy white jazz impresario, Hammond had hoped to welcome on stage Robert Johnson, the man he thought to be the greatest of all the blues singers. But when he sent an emissary to track him down in Mississippi, Hammond was startled to learn that Robert had died only months earlier.

A Voice From the Grave: Released in 1990, *The Complete Recordings* of Robert Johnson, which include alternate takes, are remastered off the best-quality original 78s available. This is the Rosetta stone of blues music—an hour and forty-five minutes of the purest Delta blues. If you want to start your own blues collection, look no further.

BIBLIOGRAPHY

Francis Davis, "Blue Walking Like a Man," *Atlantic Monthly*, April 1991.

Alan Greenberg, *Love In Vain*, DaCapo Press, 1994.

Peter Guralnick, *Searching for Robert Johnson*, Dutton, 1992.

Robert Johnson, *The Complete Recordings*, Sony, Original Release Date: 1990.

Alan Lomax, *The Land Where the Blues Began*, Bantam Doubleday Dell, 1993.

Barry Lee Pearson and Bill McCulloch, *Robert Johnson: Lost and Found*, University of Illinois Press, 2003.

Jon Michael Spencer, *Blues and Evil*, The University of Tennessee Press, 1993.

Elijah Wald, *Escaping the Delta*, HarperCollins, 2004.

Pete Welding, "Ramblin' Johnny Shines," *Living Blues* 22 (July-August 1975) and 23 (September-October 1975).